No Nonsense English

7-8 years

Contents

www.bondlearning.co.uk

Handwriting practice

Practise the joined words. Go over the grey words first. Make sure you start at the dot and follow the arrows. Then copy each word in the space underneath.

run boss mum sausage

ship tile giant quack

stall cake slugs bird

snow coffee regard flower

moon glow fierce lives

fleet prowl stroke toffee

Copy this poem in the space underneath each line.

Thirty days hath September

April, June and November

All the rest have thirty-one

Except February alone

Which has twenty-eight days clear,

And twenty-nine in each leap year

More practice? Go to www

Long vowel sounds

Words with **short** vowel sounds usually have one vowel (r**a**t, k**i**t, c**u**b).
Words with **long** vowel sounds can have:

- a **vowel**, then a **consonant** and end in **e** (r**a**t**e**, k**i**t**e**, c**u**b**e**)
- **two vowels** together (b**ai**l, m**oo**d, fr**ui**t, b**ee**, gl**ue**)
- a **vowel** and **y** (h**ay**, b**oy**, th**ey**)

1. **Underline the words with long vowel sounds and circle the words with short vowel sounds.**

   tail   pot   brick   late   sit   sleep   day   cat   away   meat   sow

   set   pie   hat   mite   cute   meet   plate   write   fit   food   lip

2. **Complete these words using ee or ea.**

   a h__ __t   **b** tr__ __   **c** b__ __d   **d** s__ __t   **e** ch__ __se

3. **Write three other words with the same long vowel sound.**

   a soak   _____   _____   _____

   b chew   _____   _____   _____

   c feet   _____   _____   _____

   d train   _____   _____   _____

4. **Fill in the missing long vowel sounds in these sentences.**

   a I cl__ __ned my t__ __th but one of them was l__ __se.

   b Harry pl__ __ed with the brush and spilled p__ __nt on the fl__ __r.

   c The b__ __t in the harb__ __r was qu__t__ rusty and old.

   d The ice cr__ __m was cold and he began to f__ __l c__ __l again.

   e Thr__ __ girls and one b__ __ went d__ __n the sl__d__.

0 Tough	OK	Got it! 15

Total

/15

More practice? Go to www

ing endings

Verbs are **doing** words. Add **ing** to say what is happening:

help / **help**ing   **carry** / **carry**ing

But if the verb:

- ends in e, **delete** the **e** and add ing:

    take / **tak**ing.

- has a short vowel sound before the last letter, **double** the **last letter** and add ing:

    h**op** / h**opp**ing.

1. **Circle the correct spelling of these verbs with ing endings.**

   a jump jumpping jumping jumpeing   **b** win winning wining wineing

   c ride ridding riding rideing   **d** knit kniting kniteing knitting

2. **Write out these verbs with the correct ing ending.**

   a pull _____   **b** hope _____   **c** say _____

   d shop _____   **e** leap _____   **f** cycle _____

3. **Write out these verbs without the ing endings.**

   a putting _____   **b** drumming _____   **c** fixing _____

   d feeling _____   **e** driving _____   **f** planning _____

4. **Complete the sentences using the correct verbs with ing endings.**

   buzz   walk   run   try

   Judith was _____ home from school when she heard a _____ noise and saw a large bee. "Oh!" she shouted, "It's _____ to sting me!" Soon, she was _____ down the road.

0			17	Total
Tough	OK	Got it!		17

le endings

Words ending with **le** sound as though they end in ul. Read these words out loud:

> bun**dle**   chuc**kle**   jun**gle**

Double consonants sometimes come before **le** endings:

> bu**bb**le   mi**dd**le   gi**gg**le

Letters that come before **le** endings are either tall letters (**ascenders**) like **b** or **d** or letters with tails (**descenders**) like **g** or **p**.

1. **Complete these words. Use each ending once.**

   ble   cle   dle   fle   gle   kle   ple   tle   zle

   a pric_ _ _   **b** bot _ _ _ _   **c** can _ _ _ _   **d** puz _ _ _ _   **e** wob _ _ _ _

   f wrig _ _ _   **g** ici _ _ _ _   **h** rip _ _ _ _   **i** ruf_ _ _

2. **Choose either ible or able to complete these words.**

   a veget _ _ _ _ _   **b** horr _ _ _ _ _   **c** reli _ _ _ _ _   **d** B _ _ _ _ _

   e prob _ _ _ _ _   **f** c _ _ _ _ _   **g** respons _ _ _ _ _   **h** ed _ _ _ _ _

3. **Complete this poem using the le words below.**

   incredible   impossible   muddle   terrible

   possible   puddle   sparkle   article

   The journalist wrote a scientific a_____
   About the way the stars shine and s_____.
   The Sun is so hot and fierce and t_____.
   At six thousand degrees it's really i_____.
   The Moon is so cold – it would be i_____.
   To live somewhere that breathing isn't p_____.
   There's no water at all, not even a p_____.
   If you tried to live there you'd be in a real m_____.

0			18
Tough	OK	Got it!	

Total

18

Prefixes 1

> **Prefixes** are groups of letters placed at the beginning of a word, which change its meaning.
>
> **pre** means **'before'**   **pre**pay – to pay beforehand
> **re** means **'again'**   **re**write – to write something again

1. **Choose the correct prefix to complete these words.**

a _____cycle   b _____place   c _____visit   d _____diction

e _____fix   f _____fill   g _____bound   h _____build

i _____cedent   j _____call   k _____mature   l _____caution

2. **Choose a prefix to complete these sentences.**

a Pascale saw the Sun's rays _____flecting off the sea.

b Oscar watched the roundabout slowly _____volve.

c John will start to _____pare for his exams tomorrow.

d Before reading the first chapter, I read the _____face.

> **QUICK TIP!**
> Use a dictionary to help you complete the words.

3. **What do you think these words mean?**

a remix _____

b preheat _____

c replay _____

d preview _____

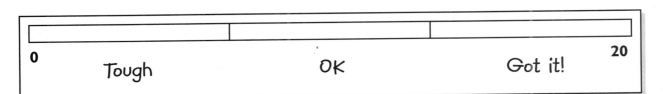

0	Tough	OK	Got it!	20

Total

/20

Prefixes 2

> Adding the prefixes **un**, **de** or **dis** changes the meaning of a word into its opposite.
> Words with opposite meanings are called **antonyms**.
>
> **un** means 'not'   **un**able – not able
> **de** means 'making the opposite of'   **de**mist – to remove mist
> **dis** means 'not' or 'the opposite of'   **dis**honest – not honest

1. **Choose the correct prefix to complete these antonyms.**

   a _____likely   **b** _____organised   **c** _____kind   **d** _____duct

   e _____trust   **f** _____form   **g** _____fit   **h** _____appear

   i _____fuse   **j** _____load   **k** _____seen   **l** _____approve

2. **Complete these sentences using the antonym of the word in bold.**

   a George said the referee's decision was **fair** but Jo said it was _____.

   b Teresa tried to _____ the **code** that Sally had written.

   c Raj tried to **connect** to the Internet but had to _____ the cable first.

   d Mary had an _____ room but Gita's was **tidy**.

3. **Complete the sentences by making antonyms for the words in brackets.**

   a It was _____ for David's Mum to collect him after school. (usual)

   b "I _____ of your choice in music," remarked Charlie. (approve)

   c The spy's mission was to _____ the computer network. (bug)

   d "I'd be _____ if I didn't support my team," said Alfie. (loyal)

0			20
Tough	OK	Got it!	

Total

/20

More practice? Go to www

Synonyms 1

> Synonyms are words that have the **same** or **similar** meanings.
> Synonyms of **big** are: huge massive gigantic enormous.
>
> Using synonyms of common words makes something more interesting to read.

1. **Make three lists of synonyms using these words.**

    dreadful   horrible   relish   miniature   small   tiny   love   awful   enjoy

    a little   _____   _____   _____

    b like   _____   _____   _____

    c nasty   _____   _____   _____

2. **Write three synonyms for these words.**

    a good _____   _____   _____

    b nice _____   _____   _____

    c said _____   _____   _____

3. **Choose a synonym to complete each sentence.**

    a Yarin was an extremely _____ boy. (clever)

    b Paul found the maths questions very _____. (hard)

    c The _____ singer was driven in a Rolls Royce. (wealthy)

    d Our school concert _____ at 7.30pm. (starts)

    e The joiner _____ the broken fence. (mended)

    > QUICK TIP!
    > Use a **thesaurus**
    > to find synonyms.

| 0 | Tough | OK | Got it! | 11 |

Total

11

More practice? Go to www

9

Verbs

Verbs tell you what is **happening** in a sentence.
They can be '**doing**' words: jump, watch, drive, read
or '**being**' words: like, know, am, is.

QUICK TIP!
Every sentence
needs a verb.

1. **Underline the verbs in these sentences.**

   a The footballer kicked the ball into the net.

   b Her cot is full of toys.

   c Amran tied his shoelaces.

   d Joe rode his bike down the path.

2. **Complete each sentence using these verbs.**

   goes   plays   waits   choose   sing   carries   walk   fly

   a Sylvie _____ in the park every day.

   b Astrid wants to _____ in an aeroplane.

   c When he _____ to school Josh _____ his bags.

   d All the children _____ songs in assembly.

   e We go to the library on Mondays to _____ our favourite books.

   f Dad _____ for me after school and then we _____ home.

3. **Write sentences using these verbs.**

   a dance _____

   b answer _____

   c suggest _____

   d hope _____

   e stop _____

0			15
Tough	OK	Got it!	

Total

/15

Similar verbs

> It is important to choose the verbs you use carefully. A verb that is similar to another might be more effective in describing what is being done.
>
> He **walked** down the street.   He **tiptoed** down the street.
>
> **Tiptoed** is **more descriptive** than **walked**.
>
> Sometimes changing the verb changes the meaning of the sentence.
>
> He **walked** down the street.   He **looked** down the street.

1. **How else could he have moved down the street?**

He walked down the street.
He ran down the street.

_____

_____

_____

_____

2. **Change the verb in these sentences to make a sentence with a similar meaning and one with a different meaning.** *(6 marks)*

a I grabbed the ball.

Similar:_____

Different:_____

b We giggled about it.

Similar:_____

Different:_____

c I slurped the lemonade.

Similar:_____

Different:_____

			Total
0 Tough	OK	Got it! 7	7

Past tense

Verbs tell you **what** is happening.

The tense of a verb tells you **when** something happened.

The **present tense** is used to show something is **happening now**.

The **past tense** is used to show something has **already happened**:

I was playing football.   or   I played football.

1. **Circle the correct past tense for these verbs.**

a	**keep**	keeped	kept	keped
b	**wash**	wash	washed	washt
c	**make**	made	maked	maid
d	**clean**	cleant	cleaned	cleans
e	**catch**	cought	catched	caught
f	**speak**	speaked	spoke	spook

2. **Choose the correct spelling of the verbs to complete these past tense sentences.**

a Adam _____ a new toy yesterday. (bought / buyed / bide)

b Penny _____ the ball. (throwed / threw / throw)

c Sher _____ down the pitch. (run / ran / runned)

d We _____ our ice creams quickly. (eated / ate / eight)

3. **Complete these sentences using the past tense of the verb.**

a Joe _____ his bike down the path. (to ride)

b Amran _____ his shoelaces. (to tie)

c I _____ playing on the beach. (to enjoy)

d My sister _____ very loudly! (to sneeze)

0			14
Tough	OK	Got it!	

Total

14

More practice? Go to

Nouns

> A **noun** is a naming word – it is used to name a **thing** or a **feeling**.
> - **Common nouns** are general names of people or things:
>   book, coat, hill, woman, town.
> - **Proper nouns** are specific names or titles of people, places or things:
>   Manchester, Prime Minister, Jenny, January, Sergeant Scott.

1. **Circle the proper nouns and underline the common nouns.**

   a Cyril went to the park on Sunday.

   b Ali lives at 2 Kenton Gardens, Hastings.

   c John's story is called 'Tiger Tom's Birthday Party'.

   d Ying's home is in China – Shanghai is his favourite city.

   e Josh's book was called 'My Friend Flipper'.

   f My friend lives in Spain.

> QUICK TIP!
> **Proper nouns** always start with a **capital letter**.

2. **Group the proper nouns in the table.**

Monday   Helena   United Kingdom   August   Wilton Crescent
Lakemede School   Professor Brown   Freddie   Paris

People			
Places			
Things			

3. **Rearrange the letters in the brackets to form a word. Decide if each word is a common or proper noun then complete the sentence.**

   a _____ had toast and cereal for her breakfast every morning. (eymil)

   b I saw my favourite _____ programme last night. (tevelisino)

   c We went to _____ for a day trip on _____. (onldon / dayuns)

   d "I am very excited! We are going on _____ next week." (ayholdi)

| 0 | Tough | OK | Got it! | 11 |

Total
☐ 11

Adjectives 1

> **Adjectives** are **describing words** – they **describe nouns**.
> The sentence
>
> 'The **red**, **yellow** and **blue** parrot was in a **golden** cage.'
>
> is more interesting and descriptive than
>
> 'The parrot was in a cage.'

1. **Use an adjective to describe each of these nouns. Use each adjective once.**

    smiley   rustling   tiny   bright   open   cloudy

    a a _____ sound   **b** a _____ sky

    c the _____ sunshine   **d** an _____ door

    e a _____ face   **f** the _____ baby

2. **Read the sentences and write the nouns and adjectives.**

Sentences	Adjectives	Nouns
a He visited his old grandmother.		
b She lived in a tiny cottage with a pretty, colourful garden.		
c The young children ate some ripe, juicy strawberries.		

3. **Circle the adjectives – there are 15 of them.**   *(15 marks)*

    It was a warm, sunny day and Jules took her little brother to the park. As
    they walked under the rustling trees they saw an ice cream seller and went to
    look at all of the ice creams. Jules chose a vanilla and chocolate cone and her
    brother had a juicy, strawberry ice lolly. They were delicious. Then Jules saw
    her best friend, Shauna, walking a fluffy, black-and-white puppy.

    "Oh!" said Jules, "Your puppy is so sweet. Can I pick him up and give him a
    big cuddle?"

    "Yes!" said Shauna. "But he might give you a wet lick!"

0			24
Tough	OK	Got it!	

Total

/ 24

More practice? Go to www

Sentences

All sentences begin with a capital letter and always end with a form of punctuation: a full stop (.), an exclamation mark (!) or question mark (?).
Names begin with a capital letter too.
Sentences are difficult to read and understand if there are no punctuation marks.

1. **Rewrite these sentences including the missing capital letters.**

   it is asim's birthday today! he is eight years old. his party is on saturday. ten of his friends are coming.

   _____

   _____

   _____

2. **Put in the missing full stops.**   (3 marks, $^1/_2$ mark for each)

   Claire lived with her Mum in a fourth floor flat She wanted a pet She really wanted a puppy to take for a walk Her Mum said that a budgie would be a better pet to have in a flat This made Claire upset She couldn't take a budgie for a walk

3. **Rewrite these sentences correctly.**

   Do
   a ~~do~~ mr and mrs smith live in the united kingdom

   _____

   b doctor and professor jones are from the united states

   _____

   c tracey and neil brown are going to florida for their holiday

   _____

0			7	Total
Tough	OK	Got it!		⧄ 7

Question and exclamation marks

> If a **question** is being asked, a sentence ends with a **question mark**.
>
> Do you want some milk?
>
> To exclaim means to **shout** or **cry out**. A sentence ends with an **exclamation mark** to express an order or an emotion such as surprise, fear or pleasure.
>
> Stop!　　Wait!　　Fantastic!　　That was amazing!

1. **Finish these sentences with a question mark or full stop.**

   a Can we go to the circus on Saturday, Mum __

   b If we leave now we will get to the shops before they close __

   c Why can't I __

   d Are you sure that it is Millie's birthday today __

   e I don't think you meant to say that __

2. **Finish these sentences with an exclamation mark or full stop.**

   a We can go to the match when you have done your homework __

   b Stop __ Thief __

   c Sara opened the curtains when she got out of bed __

   d What a beautiful day __

   e No__ Don't __ You could hurt yourself __

3. **Fill in the gaps using the correct punctuation.**　　(11 marks)

   Dad__ Mum__ Help__ Can you hear me__ I climbed up into this tree and now

   I am stuck__ Can you come and get me down__ Hurry__ Are you coming__

   I think you'll need to get a ladder__ Thanks__ It was scary up there__

0			21
Tough	OK	Got it!	

Total

21

More practice?　Go to www

Speech marks

> **Speech marks** show that someone is speaking. They go at the beginning and end of what is being said.
>
> "Hurry up or we'll be late," shouted Dad.
>
> Rosie called downstairs, "I'm just coming."
>
> A **capital letter** is needed when someone begins to speak.
> If the **comma** is **after** what is spoken it goes **inside** the speech marks.
> If the **comma** is **before** what is spoken it goes **outside** the speech marks.

1. Write the speech marks in these sentences.

a It's snowing, cried Eamon.

b We could go outside and build a snowman, suggested Shannon.

c Mum laughed, There's not enough snow!

d But I don't mind if it's a tiny snowman, Eamon pleaded.

2. Rewrite these sentences. Use capital letters, commas, speech marks and full stops.

a it's Katie's birthday party tonight whispered Sophie

_____

b i'm really looking forward to it replied Amy

_____

c Emma leaned over and interrupted what are you going to wear?

_____

d I might wear my new jeans Sophie replied

_____

0			8	Total
Tough	OK	Got it!		8

How are stories organised?

All stories have a beginning, a middle and an end.
The **beginning** tells you where the story starts and introduces the main characters.
In the **middle** of the story something happens.
The **end** or **resolution** finishes the story.

1. **Read this short story then answer the questions.**

Claire wanted a pet. She wanted a puppy to take for walks, or a cat to curl up on her lap, or a rabbit so she could stroke its soft fur, or a budgie that could talk.

Claire kept on talking about having a pet. One night her Mum made a suggestion. "Why don't you find out about the pets you might like, and why, then we can talk about it again?"

"Thanks, Mum!" exclaimed Claire, giving her a big hug. She found out about different pets at the library. She decided on a rabbit.

a Underline the key sentence that describes the beginning of the story.

b Underline the key sentence that describes the middle of the story.

c Underline the key sentence that describes the end of the story.

d Do you think Claire was given a pet? _____

e Write a sentence that explains your answer.

_____

_____

2. **Tick those phrases that could be used to start a story. Put a cross against those that could end a story.**

a Once upon a time there lived a magic rabbit. ____

b They never went there again. ____

c It all began a long time ago. ____

d The other day I went to the seaside. ____

e That was the last we saw of him! ____

f They lived in a beautiful castle and lived happily ever after. ____

g Things were quite different when I was young. ____

h Everyone shouted, "Hooray!" ____

3. **Read these sentences from the middle of a story, then put them in the correct order.**

    a Luke whispered back, "I know a way".

    b They crept silently down the stairs to the front door.

    c He climbed on to the wide windowsill and undid the window's catch.

    d "How are we going to get out?" whispered Jerry.

    e It was locked and bolted.

    _____

4. **Write an ending to this story. It must finish the story properly.**

Patrick was worried. He hadn't seen Ciaran for three days.

    "I wonder what's happened to him?" he puzzled. "It's not like him to just go off and disappear. Something must be wrong."

Patrick walked over to Ciaran's house, but the windows were closed and the doors were locked. He peered through the letterbox and saw a pile of envelopes on the floor. The house hadn't been lived in for days.

_____

_____

_____

_____

_____

_____

_____

_____

_____

_____

Reading information

Fiction is the term we use to refer to stories and poems that are made up and describe imaginary events and people.

Non-fiction is the term we use to refer to all kinds of writing that describe information and facts about real things. Lists, official letters, notes, labels, diaries, instructions and signs are all examples of non-fiction.

---

1.   Read Shamilka's after-school diary and then answer the questions.

Monday	Tuesday	Wednesday	Thursday	Friday	Saturday	Sunday
Maths homework	Literacy homework	Science homework	Spelling homework			Check homework is finished
	Book club	Guitar lesson			Swimming	

    a When has Shamilka got Science homework? _____

    b Which day is the book club? _____

    c Are there any days when she has no homework? _____

    d What does she do on Mondays? _____

    e When does she check her homework? _____

2.   Read the passage and use the information to complete Bryn's timetable.   *(6 marks)*

Monday	Tuesday	Wednesday	Thursday	Friday	Saturday	Sunday

Bryn was running late, as usual. "Oh no!" he said, "I've forgotten my kit and we always have football on Tuesdays and Thursdays."

    "That's right," called his Mum, "But don't forget you've got your dentist appointment this Tuesday, so you'll have to miss football. And remember that you've got to practise your flute on Friday before your lesson on Saturday."

    Bryn scowled. He hated the dentist. But at least if he wasn't playing football he'd have time to finish the Maths homework he started on Monday. "I'll play football on Sunday with Dad instead," he said.

    "No!" shouted his Mum. "I told you! We're going to Auntie Jean's barbeque on Sunday."

3. **Read this recipe for Apple Stripeys.**

Apple Stripeys are my Mum's favourite dessert! Before you start slicing up the apples, you'll need to make sure that you've peeled them with a vegetable peeler and thrown away the cores.

You'll need two large or three small apples for this recipe, as well as some double cream to whip with a rotary whisk and some ginger biscuits.

Use a sharp knife to slice the apples, then spread the whipped cream onto one side of the ginger biscuits and put a slice of apple on top. Keep going like this until you've used up all the biscuits and apple slices. Then wrap them in some tin foil and put in the fridge over night.

When you get the rest of the whipped cream out the next day, use a teaspoon to spread it over the apple and ginger slices. You'll have delicious Apple Stripeys!

And don't forget, knives are sharp, so be careful when you're slicing!

Turn the recipe into a set of instructions. Write them in the correct order. Start like this:

Ingredients _____

Kitchen tools _____

Instructions _Peel the apples_ _____

_____

_____

_____

_____

_____

(7 marks)

How am I doing?

1. **Write two other words with the same long vowels.**

   a faint _____ _____   **b** meat _____ _____

   c meet _____ _____   **d** arrive _____ _____

   e lies _____ _____

2. **Correctly add ing to these verbs.**

   a slide _____   **b** pump _____   **c** pop _____

3. **Write these verbs taking away the ing ending.**

   a shaving _____   **b** sailing _____   **c** patting _____

4. **Choose the correct le ending to complete these words.**

   able   ible   ple   ble   tle   kle   zle   dle

   a horr_____   **b** improb_____   **c** ap_____   **d** daz_____

   e rum_____   **f** ket_____   **g** an_____   **h** mud_____

5. **Add the prefix pre or re to complete these words.**

   a _____diction   **b** _____cedent   **c** _____duction   **d** _____visit

6. **Choose the prefix un, de or dis to complete these antonyms.**

   a _____able   **b** _____mist   **c** _____loyal   **d** _____important

   e _____form   **f** _____likely   **g** _____trust   **h** _____camp

7. **Make three groups of synonyms.**

   hysterical   silent   peaceful   intelligent   hilarious   brilliant

   a quiet _____

   b funny _____

   c clever _____

8. **Change the verb in this sentence to make a sentence with a similar meaning and one with a different meaning.** *(2 marks)*

I called after him.

Similar:_____

Different:_____

9. **Choose the correct past tense of these verbs.**

   a The ducklings _____ after their mother. (swimmed / swam / swimming)

   b Mum _____ her car to work yesterday. (drove / droved / drived / drive)

   c Jason _____ really happy this morning. (is / am / was / were)

10. **Circle the proper nouns and underline the common nouns.**

   a Mrs Johnson parked her car in the car park and went to the shops.

   b I met Gloria and David when I went to the cinema to watch the film.

   c The address is 16 Farmhouse Avenue, Stanton, Oxfordshire.

11. **Circle the adjectives in these sentences.**

   a The furious wind howled and the little old chimney pots shivered and rattled.

   b The icy cold rain pounded on the ancient castle's crumbly walls.

   c The beautiful, warm sun shone on the lush green grass.

12. **Punctuate these sentences correctly. Look for missing full stops, speech marks and capital letters.**

   a megan and her sister live at 24 green street in hastings last christmas they went to london to see cinderella

   b it's time for bed said mum

   please can I stay up a bit longer pleaded archie

   mum sighed ok, but only for 10 minutes

Total

47

More practice? Go to www

Suffixes: er and est

Suffixes are groups of letters placed at the end of a word.
The word endings **er** and **est** are used to compare one thing with another.

For most words the spelling doesn't change when you add **er** or **est**.

   cold   **cold**er   **cold**est

But for some words the spelling does change before you add the suffix. If the word

- ends in **e**, delete the **e**.
- ends in **y**, change the **y** into **i**.
- has a **short vowel** sound, **double** the last letter.

ripe / rip**er** / rip**est**
happy / happ**ier** / happ**iest**
hot / ho**tter** / ho**ttest**

1. **Add the endings er and est to these words.**

   a rich_____ _____   **b** nice_____ _____

   c chilly_____ _____   **d** quick_____ _____

   e rude_____ _____   **f** close_____ _____

   g tall_____ _____   **h** tiny_____ _____

2. **Write the missing short vowel sound words.**

   a   big   _____   biggest   **b** _____ _____ wettest

   c _____ thinner _____   **d** red _____ _____

3. **Write the correct spelling for these words.**

   a crazyest _____   **b** greatter _____   **c** lateest _____

   d quiettest _____   **e** fitest _____   **f** funnyer _____

0			18
Tough	OK	Got it!	

Total
18

More practice? Go to www

Suffixes: y

To turn some nouns into adjectives, add the suffix **y**.

For most words the spelling doesn't change when you add **y**.

trick   **trick**y

But for some words the spelling does change. If the word

- ends in **e**, delete the **e**.   mous**e** / mous**y**
- has a **short vowel** sound, **double** the last letter.   **cat** / ca**tty**

1. Change these nouns into adjectives by adding y.

a cheek _____   b prickle _____   c crisp _____

d fur _____   e grease _____   f water _____

g chill _____   h wit _____   i haze _____

j chat _____   k fog _____   l noise _____

2. Write these adjectives as nouns.

a leafy _____   b funny _____   c slimy _____   d fussy _____

e ~~potty~~ _____   f lazy _____   g nutty _____   h shiny _____

3. Change the nouns in brackets to adjectives and complete the sentences.

It had been a _____ (sun) day but now it was a _____

(star) night and it was quite _____ (mist) near the ground. I could

see two _____ (stripe) badgers coming across the field. Their

home was in the _____ (hill) bank right beside me, an

_____ (earth) den.

			Total
0 Tough	OK	Got it! 21	/21

More practice? Go to www

Plural nouns

Singular means one of something and plural means more than one of something. Many singular nouns are made into plural nouns by adding **s**.

cat / cat**s**

But for nouns ending in

- **s**, **ss**, **sh**, **ch** or **x** add **es**.   chur**ch** / chur**ches**   bo**x** / bo**xes**
- **o** add **s** or **es**.   radi**o** / radi**os**   tomat**o** / tomat**oes**
- a **consonant** and **y**, change **y** to an **i** and add **es**.   bab**y** / bab**ies**

QUICK TIP!
Add s to musical instruments ending in o.

1. **Write the plurals for these nouns.**

a potato _____   **b** gas _____   **c** piano _____

d ape _____   **e** brush _____   **f** fox _____

g match _____   **h** case _____   **i** wish _____

j circus _____   **k** cello _____   **l** table _____

2. **Write the plurals for these nouns.**

a monkey _____   **b** holiday _____   **c** puppy _____

d berry _____   **e** ray _____   **f** party _____

Some nouns do not follow these rules. They have irregular plurals and just have to be learnt.

child / child**ren**

3. **Write the singular form of these irregular plural nouns.**

a men _____   **b** people _____   **c** geese _____

d feet _____   **e** mice _____   **f** oxen _____

0			24
Tough	OK	Got it!	

Total

24

More practice? Go to www

Silent letters

There are lots of words that have **silent letters**. In the word **comb**, the letter **b** is silent.

Silent letters follow patterns:

- Silent **b** can come **after m** (la**m**b) and **before t** (dou**b**t).
- Silent **w** can come **before r** (**w**rite) and **after s** (s**w**ord).
- Silent **g** or **k** can come **before n** (**g**nat, **k**nife).
- Silent **l** can come **after** the vowels **a**, **o** and **ou** (ca**l**m / yo**l**k / sho**ul**d).
- Silent **h** can come **after r** (r**h**ythm) and **after w** (w**h**en).

1.   Underline the silent letters in these words.

thumb   debt   wrap   answer   gnash   knot   balm   rhubarb

rhyme   which   would   folk   wrist   crumb   knock   wring

2.   Complete these words using silent letters.

a __nead   **b** bom__   **c** __nome   **d** ha__f

e __nuckle   **f** __rinkle   **g** __now   **h** w__eat

i __nee   **j** __nit   **k** cha__k   **l** __reck

3.   Add a silent letter to the letters in brackets and complete these sentences.

a The _____ fought the dragon and rescued the princess. (night)

b Hamsters like to _____ on pieces of wood. (naw)

c Sally got three questions _____ in her English test. (rong)

d Farmer McDonald went to see the new _____ in the cow shed. (caf)

e Timothy went on a boat trip to see the _____. (wales)

			Total
0			18
Tough	OK	Got it!	18

More practice? Go to

Compound words

Compound words are made when two or three small words are joined together to make one longer one.

in + side = **inside**   work + man + ship = **workmanship**

Compound words usually have a different meaning to the individual words.

1.   Join the words and write the compound words they make.

play	lace	_playground_	bed	bin	_____
air	ground	_____	wind	house	_____
week	keeper	_____	dust	work	_____
shoe	port	_____	green	mill	_____
goal	end	_____	fire	room	_____

2.   Write two compound words that start with each of the words below.

a rain _____ _____

b farm _____ _____

c post _____ _____

d snow _____ _____

e water _____ _____

QUICK TIP!
Use a dictionary
if you get stuck.

3.   Make the words below into compound nouns and put them into the sentences.

board   up   cup   fast   ship   crafts   stairs

break   man   grand   noon   after   mother

a In the morning we eat _____ .

b Mum dried the plate and put it in the _____ .

c "This table is an excellent example of good _____ ."

d Dad sent them _____ to bed.

e Sam went to see his _____ on Saturday _____ .

QUICK TIP!
Cross off the
words as you
use them.

0			19
Tough	OK	Got it!	

Total

/19

More practice? Go to www

28

Suffixes: ly, ful, less

Spelling | Lesson 22

The suffix **ly** means 'in this manner'.

    kind**ly**   – in a kind manner / acting in a kind way

The suffix **ful** means 'full of' and the suffix **less** means 'without'.

    hopeful   – full of hope
    hopeless   – without hope

The spelling of most words does not need to be changed to add these suffixes.
But if the word **ends** in **y**, change the **y** to **i** and then add **ly**.

---

1. **Write the new words made when you add ly to these words.**

   a real _____   **b** proper _____   **c** actual _____

   d like _____   **e** friend _____   **f** slow _____

   g rapid_____   **h** original _____   **i** eventual _____

2. **Add the suffixes ful and less to these words.**   *(5 marks, ¹/₂ mark for each)*

	ful	less
a pity		
b thank		
c use		
d care		
e pain		

3. **Write the new words made when you add ly, ful or less to these words.**

   a friend _____   **b** wish _____   **c** care _____

   d home _____   **e** week _____   **f** forget _____

   g pain _____   **h** thank _____   **i** usual _____

			Total
0 Tough	OK	Got it! ²³	/23

More practice? Go to **www**

Adjectives 2

Some adjectives describe **colour** – red, blue, lilac.
Others describe **size** – large, small, gigantic.
They can also describe **moods** and **feelings** – happy, enthusiastic, sad.

Choosing adjectives carefully can help someone more clearly imagine what is being described.

1. **Write the adjectives in the correct columns in the table.**   *(3 marks)*

| orange | huge | green | tiny | carefree | enormous |
| medium | cross | pink | black | miserable | cheerful |

Colour	Size	Mood

2. **Include as many of the adjectives from question 1 as possible in a short story of your own.**

_____

_____

_____

_____

_____

_____

_____

_____

0			4
Tough	OK	Got it!	

Total

More practice? Go to www

Singular and plural sentences

To change a sentence from **singular** (one) to **plural** (more than one), all parts of the sentence must agree.

Singular: Simon has **a car**.   Plural: Simon has **two cars**.

Singular: **John plays** football.   Plural: **John and Tom play** football.

1. Change these sentences from singular to plural.

a Jesse enjoys writing and likes reading books.

Jesse and Jamal _____

b Kalisha liked walking until she got a bicycle. Now she likes cycling.

Kalisha and Oman _____

c Jeff used to learn French, but now he learns Spanish instead.

Jeff and Joy _____

d I am going swimming on Saturday before I go shopping.

We _____

2. Change these sentences from plural to singular.

a Tessa and Brady swim in the school team and also play tennis.

Tessa _____

b We used to sing in the choir but Shona and I now sing solo.

I _____

c "Have you seen Colin and Jason? They are late for PE!"

"Have you seen Colin? _____

d I have three cats, two dogs and a rabbit but my favourite pet is the rabbit.

I have one _____

			Total
0		8	
Tough	OK	Got it!	8

More practice? Go to www

31

Collective nouns

> **Collective nouns** are words used to describe a **collection** or **group** of things.
>
> a **flock** of sheep   a **crowd** of people

1. **Match the collective nouns to the correct animals and birds.**

litter   herd   gaggle   pack   flock   flight   shoal   swarm

a a ___herd___ of elephants   **b** a ___flock___ of sheep

c a ___litter___ of pigs lers   **d** a ___shoal___ of fish

e a ___gaggle___ of geese   **f** a ___pack___ of wolves

g a ___swarm___ of bees   **h** a ___flight___ of birds

2. **Join the collective nouns to the people they describe and write the phrases.**

a a cast of   directors   _____

b a tribe of   actors   _____

c a board of   sailors   _____

d a crew of   natives   _____

3. **Use the correct collective noun to complete each of these sentences.**

batch   deck   brood   bunch   clutch   galaxy

a A ___batch___ of loaves came straight out of the oven.

b On a clear night you can see a ___galaxy___ of stars in the sky.

c Lara saw a ___clutch___ of eggs in the blackbird's nest.

d A ___brood___ of hens were sitting on their nests.

e Dad bought a large _____ of bananas from the market stall.

f Stuart shuffled the _____ of cards before dealing them out.

> **QUICK TIP!**
> Tick the words
> as you use them.

0			18
Tough	OK	Got it!	

Total

18

More practice? Go to www

No Nonsense
English

7-8 years

Parents' notes

What your child will learn from this book

Bond No Nonsense will help your child to understand and become more confident at English. This book features the main English objectives covered by your child's class teacher during the school year. It provides clear, straightforward teaching and learning of the essentials in a rigorous, step-by-step way.

This book begins with some **handwriting practice**. Encourage your child to complete this carefully and to continue writing neatly throughout the book.

The four types of lessons provided are:
Spelling – these cover spelling rules and strategies.
Grammar – these cover word types and sentence construction.
Punctuation – these cover punctuation marks and their rules.
Comprehension – these cover reading different types of text and comprehension questions.

How you can help

Following a few simple guidelines will ensure that your child gets the best from this book:
- Explain that the book will help your child become confident in their English work.
- If your child has difficulty reading the text on the page or understanding a question, do provide help.
- Encourage your child to complete all the exercises in a lesson. You can mark the work using this answer section (which you will also find on the website). Your child can record their own impressions of the work using the 'How did I do' feature.

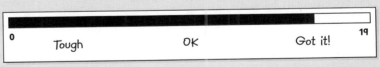

0			19
Tough	OK	Got it!	

- The 'How am I doing?' sections provide a further review of progress.

Using the website – www.bondlearning.co.uk
- The website provides extra practice of every skill in the book. So if your child does not feel confident about a lesson, they can go to the website and have another go.
- For every page of this book you will find further practice questions and their answers available to download.
- To access the extra practice pages:
  1. Go to www.bondlearning.co.uk
  2. Click on 'English'
  3. Click on '7–8 Years'
  4. Click on the lesson you want.

Bond No Nonsense 7–8 years Answers

① Long vowel sounds p4

1 Long: tail late sleep day away meat sow pie mite cute meet plate write food
Short: pot brick sit cat set hat fit lip

2 **a** heat **b** tree **c** bead **d** seat **e** cheese

3 Possible answers include:
a coat boat loan **b** threw blew mews **c** neat meet wheat
d plain plane crane

4 **a** cleaned / teeth / loose **b** played / paint / floor **c** boat / harbour / quite
d cream / feel / cool **e** Three / boy / down / slide

② ing endings p5

1 **a** jumping **b** winning **c** riding **d** knitting
2 **a** pulling **b** hoping **c** saying **d** shopping
e leaping **f** cycling
3 **a** put **b** drum **c** fix **d** feel
e drive **f** plan
4 walking / buzzing / trying / running

③ le endings p6

1 **a** prickle **b** bottle **c** candle **d** puzzle **e** wobble
f wriggle **g** icicle **h** ripple **i** ruffle
2 **a** vegetable **b** horrible **c** reliable **d** Bible **e** probable
f cable **g** responsible **h** edible
3 article / sparkle / terrible / incredible / impossible / possible / puddle / muddle

④ Prefixes 1 p7

1 **a** re **b** re **c** re **d** pre **e** pre **f** re
g re **h** re **i** pre **j** re **k** pre **l** pre
2 **a** re **b** re **c** pre **d** pre
3 **a** mix again **b** heat before
c play again **d** view before

⑤ Prefixes 2 p8

1 **a** unlikely **b** disorganised **c** unkind **d** deduct
e distrust **f** deform **g** unfit **h** disappear
i defuse **j** unload **k** unseen **l** disapprove
2 **a** unfair **b** decode **c** disconnect **d** untidy
3 **a** unusual **b** disapprove **c** debug **d** disloyal

⑥ Synonyms 1 p9

1 **a** little / small / miniature / tiny
b like / enjoy / relish / love
c nasty / dreadful / awful / horrible
2 Possible answers include:
a great fantastic excellent **b** lovely wonderful fantastic
c uttered shouted whispered
3 Possible answers include:
a intelligent **b** difficult **c** rich **d** begins
e fixed

⑦ Verbs p10

1 **a** kicked **b** is **c** tied **d** rode
2 **a** plays **b** fly **c** goes/carries **d** sing
e choose **f** waits walk
3 Answers will vary.

⑧ Similar verbs p11

1 Answers will vary.
2 Answers will vary.

⑨ Past tense p12

1 **a** kept **b** washed **c** made **d** cleaned **e** caught
f spoke
2 **a** bought **b** threw **c** ran **d** ate
3 **a** rode **b** tied **c** enjoyed **d** sneezed

⑩ Nouns p13

1 **a** (Cyril) went to the (park) on (Sunday).
b (Ali) lives at 2 (Kenton Gardens), (Hastings).
c (John's) (story) is called (Tiger Tom's Birthday Party).
d (Ying's) (home) is in (China) – (Shanghai) is his favourite (city).
e (Josh's) (book) was called (My Friend Flipper).
f My (friend) lives in (Spain).
2 People: Helena, Professor Brown, Freddie
Places: United Kingdom, Wilton Crescent, Paris
Things: Monday, August, Lakemede School
3 **a** Emily **b** television **c** London/Sunday **d** holiday

⑪ Adjectives 1 p14

1 **a** rustling **b** cloudy **c** bright **d** open **e** smiley **f** tiny
2 **a** Adjectives: old Nouns: grandmother
b Adjectives: tiny, pretty, colourful Nouns: cottage, garden
c Adjectives: young, ripe, juicy Nouns: children, strawberries
3 warm, sunny, little, rustling, vanilla, chocolate, juicy, strawberry, delicious, best,
fluffy, black-and-white, sweet, big, wet

⑫ Sentences p15

1 It is Asim's birthday today! He is eight years old. His party is on Saturday. Ten of his
friends are coming.
2 Claire lived with her Mum in a fourth floor flat. She wanted a pet. She really wanted
a puppy to take for a walk. Her Mum said that a budgie would be a better pet to
have in a flat. This made Claire upset. She couldn't take a budgie for a walk.
3 **a** Do Mr and Mrs Smith live in the United Kingdom?
b Doctor and Professor Jones are from the United States.
c Tracey and Neil Brown are going to Florida for their holiday.

⑬ Question and exclamation marks p16

1 **a** ? **b** . **c** ? **d** ? **e** .
2 **a** . **b** !/! **c** . **d** ! **e** !/!/.
3 !/!/!/?/./?/!/?/./!/.

⑭ Speech marks p17

1 **a** "It's snowing," cried Eamon.
b "We could go outside and build a snowman," suggested Shannon.
c Mum laughed, "There's not enough snow!"
d "But I don't mind if it's a tiny snowman," Eamon pleaded.
2 **a** "It's Katie's birthday party tonight," whispered Sophie.
b "I'm really looking forward to it," replied Amy.
c Emma leaned over and interrupted, "What are you going to wear?"
d "I might wear my new jeans," Sophie replied.

⑮ How are stories organised? p18

1 **a** Claire wanted a pet.
b Claire kept on talking about having a pet.
c She decided on a rabbit.
d Yes
e Claire had read about different pets to find out which one would be best for her.
2 **a** ✓ **b** ✗ **c** ✓ **d** ✓ **e** ✗ **f** ✗
g ✓ **h** ✗
3 b e d a c
4 Answers will vary.

⑯ Reading information p20

1 **a** Wednesday **b** Tuesday **c** Friday, Saturday, Sunday
d Maths homework **e** Sunday
2 Monday: Maths homework Friday: Flute practice
Tuesday: Dentist / Maths homework Saturday: Flute lesson
Wednesday: None Sunday: Auntie Jean's barbecue
Thursday: Football
3 Ingredients: 2 to 3 apples, whipped double cream and ginger biscuits.
Kitchen tools: vegetable peeler, rotary whisk, sharp knife, tin foil and a teaspoon.
Instructions:
a Peel, core and slice the apples and whip the cream.
b Spread one side of a ginger biscuit with cream and 'sandwich' it with a slice of
apple.
c Continue until all the biscuits and apple slices are used up. (Remember to save
some whipped cream!)
d Wrap in tin foil and leave in the fridge overnight.
e Spread the rest of the whipped cream over the biscuits / apples.

How am I doing? p22

1 Possible answers include:
a paint / pain **b** bean / seat **c** feet / bee **d** chive / ride
e pies / flies
2 **a** sliding **b** pumping **c** popping
3 **a** shave **b** sail **c** pat
4 **a** horrible **b** improbable **c** apple **d** dazzle
e rumble **f** kettle **g** ankle **h** muddle
5 **a** prediction **b** precedent **c** reduction **d** revisit
6 **a** unable **b** demist **c** disloyal **d** unimportant
e deform **f** unlikely **g** distrust **h** decamp
7 **a** quiet / silent / peaceful **b** funny / hysterical / hilarious
c clever / intelligent / brilliant
8 Answers will vary.
9 **a** swam **b** drove **c** was
10 **a** (Mrs Johnson) parked her (car) in the (car park) and went to the (shops).
b I met (Gloria) and (David) and I went to the (cinema) to watch the (film).
c The (address) is 16 (Farmhouse Avenue), (Stanton), (Oxfordshire).
11 **a** furious, little, old
b icy, cold, ancient, crumbly
c beautiful, warm, lush, green
12 **a** Megan and her sister live at 24 Green Steet in Hastings. Last Christmas they went
to London to see Cinderella.
b "It's time for bed," said Mum.
"Please can I stay up a bit longer?" pleaded Archie.
Mum sighed, "OK, but only for 10 minutes."

17 Suffixes: er and est p24

1 **a** richer / richest **b** nicer / nicest **c** chillier / chilliest
   d quicker / quickest **e** ruder / rudest **f** closer / closest
   g taller / tallest **h** tinier / tiniest
2 **a** bigger **b** wet / wetter **c** thin / thinnest **d** redder / reddest
3 **a** craziest **b** greater **c** latest **d** quietest
   e fittest **f** funnier

18 Suffixes: y p25

1 **a** cheeky **b** prickly **c** crispy **d** furry
   e greasy **f** watery **g** chilly **h** witty
   i hazy **j** chatty **k** foggy **l** noisy
2 **a** leaf **b** fun **c** slime **d** fuss
   e pot **f** laze **g** nut **h** shine
3 sunny / starry / misty / stripey / hilly / earthy

19 Plural nouns p26

1 **a** potatoes **b** gases **c** pianos **d** apes **e** brushes
   f foxes **g** matches **h** cases **i** wishes **j** circuses
   k cellos **l** tables
2 **a** monkeys **b** holidays **c** puppies **d** berries **e** rays
   f parties
3 **a** man **b** person **c** goose **d** foot **e** mouse
   f ox

20 Silent letters p27

1 thumb / debt / wrap / answer / gnash / knot / balm / rhubarb / rhyme / which /
   would / folk / wrist / crumb / knock / wring
2 **a** k **b** b **c** g **d** l **e** k
   f w **g** k **h** h **i** k **j** k
   k l **l** w
3 **a** knight **b** gnaw **c** wrong **d** calf **e** whales

21 Compound words p28

1 airport / weekend / shoelace / goalkeeper / bedroom / windmill / dustbin /
   greenhouse / firework
2 Possible answers include:
   a rainbow / raindrop / rainforest **b** farmhouse / farmhand / farmyard
   c postman / postcode / postbox **d** snowman / snowball / snowflake
   e waterfall / watercolour / watercress
3 **a** breakfast **b** cupboard **c** craftsmanship
   d upstairs **e** grandmother / afternoon

22 Suffixes: ly, ful, less p29

1 **a** really **b** properly **c** actually **d** likely
   e friendly **f** slowly **g** rapidly **h** originally
   i eventually
2 **a** pitiful / pitiless **b** thankful / thankless **c** useful / useless
   d careful / careless **e** painful / painless
3 **a** friendly **b** wishful **c** careful / careless
   d homely / homeless **e** weekly **f** forgetful
   g painful / painless **h** thankful / thankless **i** usually

23 Adjectives 2 p30

1 Colour: orange / green / pink / black
   Size: huge / tiny / enormous / medium
   Mood: carefee / cross / miserable / cheerful
2 Answers will vary.

24 Singlular and plural sentences p31

1 **a** Jesse and Jamal enjoy writing and like reading books.
   b Kalisha and Oman walked until they got bicycles. Now they like cycling.
   c Jeff and Joy used to learn French, but now they learn Spanish instead.
   d We are going swimming on Saturday before we go shopping.
2 **a** Tessa swims in the school team and she also plays tennis.
   b I used to sing in the choir but I now sing solo.
   c "Have you seen Colin? He is late for PE!"
   d I have one cat, one dog and one rabbit but my favourite pet is the rabbit.

25 Collective nouns p32

1 **a** herd **b** flock **c** litter **d** shoal
   e gaggle **f** pack **g** swarm **h** flight
2 **a** a cast of actors **b** a board of directors
   c a tribe of natives **d** a crew of sailors
3 **a** batch **b** galaxy **c** clutch **d** brood
   e bunch **f** deck

26 Essential words p33

1 Verbs: go / have to remember / take / reminds / take / need / is
   Adjectives: early / blue / PE / football / favourite / whole
2 favourite
3 Last summer I went to Spain ~~with my Mum and Uncle Henry, my brother Simon~~
   ~~and sister Benita.~~ My whole family went! It was so hot, ~~I was boiling and the sun~~
   ~~shone every day.~~ It was great to go swimming in the ~~cool, blue~~ sea but Benita just
   preferred to sunbathe ~~on the beach~~.

27 1st, 2nd and 3rd person 1 p34

1 **b** second person **c** first person **d** first person
   e second person **f** third person
2 **a** We took the dog for a walk.
   b I got dressed for school very quickly.
   c I fed the ducks in the park.
   d We took turns to use the computer.

28 Commas 1 p35

1 **a** It was a tall, dark and gloomy house.
   b Mark crunched his way across the cold, frosty and sparkling field.
   c Zoe had a furry, cuddly bear for her birthday.
2 **a** The train called at Sunbury, Hampton and Fulwell.
   b The leaves in Autumn are red, yellow, gold and brown.
   c Butter, flour, sugar and a pinch of salt were the recipe's ingredients.
3 Lucas had lost Oscar. "Is he at the Town Hall, the station or the shops?" wondered
   Lucas. He tried the Town Hall, the bus terminus and last of all the market to find
   him. He found him sitting quietly by the fish stall. Oscar was eating a chunk of cod,
   a piece of haddock and some salmon!

29 Capital letters p36

1 **a** section 3: the history of the human race.
   b table of contents.
   c act 1 scene 1: pandora's house.
2 **a** Elizabethan **b** Liverpudlian **c** African
   d Japanese **e** British
3 Charlie Junior, a small baboon,
   Went outside in the great monsoon.
   When he got home he started to sneeze
   And the shivers and shakes went down to his knees.

30 Contractions 1 p37

1 **a** you'd **b** she'd **c** they'd **d** I've **e** you've
   f she's **g** I'll **h** they'll **i** you'll
2 they'll / they will it does not / it doesn't
   we are / we're I had not / I hadn't
   I am / I'm they shouldn't / they should not
3 **a** she'll **b** Here's / weren't **c** wasn't / can't
   d shouldn't have / It's **e** who'd **f** Aren't / I'm
   g it's / mustn't

31 Adventure stories p38

1 **a** In a wood **b** two **c** He can't see the path
   d A doctor **e** He wags his tail
2 Yes, because he knew Harry's name.
3 **a** leaf-strewn path **b** narrow path **c** trees leaning in
4 **b** He got lost. **c** He was found. **d** He was taken home.
5 Possible answers include:
   Foolish because he knew he wasn't meant to go for walks on his own.
6 Possible answers include:
   Frightened / panicked – the text says that: 'Harry was cold and scared.'
7 Possible answers include:
   To do as he's told.

32 Instructions p40

1 6
2 A cardboard cylinder; pieces of shiny card; 2 pieces of grease-proof paper; coloured
   shapes, e.g. sequins; an elastic band; a pencil; a pair of scissors; glue.
3 A Y-shape.
4 Shiny or reflective card.
5 With an elastic band.
6 sequins
7 Hold it to the light, look down it and rotate the tube.
8 Answers will vary.

How am I doing? p42

1 **a** fresher / freshest **b** riper / ripest **c** friendlier / friendliest
2 **a** smoky **b** crispy **c** fully **d** stony **e** watery
   f bony
3 **a** dishes **b** mice **c** feet **d** pennies **e** haloes
   f taxis
4 **a** w **b** b **c** w **d** g **e** k
   f l **g** l **h** h **i** d **j** k
5 Possible answers include:
   a sandstorm / sandcastle / sandbag **b** bedtime / bedroom / bedspread
   c bookcase / bookmark / bookshelf **d** sideboard / sideburns / sidecar
6 **a** beautiful **b** cowardly **c** powerless
7 Answers will vary.
8 **a** The men enjoy watching comedy films.
   b Justin and I think skateboarding is fun but we prefer watching it on TV.
9 **a** team, crowd **b** queue, batch **c** collection, tribes
10 **a** third person **b** second person
    c third person **d** first person
11 **a** Today has been wet, miserable and horrible.
    b Jack's puppy was cute, friendly and fully.
12 **a** needn't **b** won't **c** there's
    d you'll **e** who'd **f** I'd

33 Words inside words p44

1 **a** money **b** donkey **c** fancy **d** husband
   e sand **f** single **g** minimal **h** singer
2 Many: man / an / any them: the / he / hem spelling: in
   words: or Finding: fin / in / din / in especially: all
   smaller: all them: the / he / hem they: the / he
   words: or helps: he long: on
   hidden: hi / hid / den with: wit / it difficult: if
   inside: in your: you
   a 15 **b** 15

3
a falling: fall / all / in
b splendid: lend / end / did
c finale: fin / final / in / ale
d hindrance: hind / in / ran / an
e abundance: bun / an / dance
f admittance: ad / admit / it / tan / an
g supplement: sup / supple / up / men
h fantastic: fan / an / ant / as / tic
i obsession: obsess / on
j centimetre: cent / Tim / time / met / metre
k potatoes: pot / potato / at / to / toe / toes
l another: an / no / not / other / the / he / her

(34) Syllables p45
1 **a** rhu / barb
b ex / change
c es / cape
d sand / wich / es
e dis / ap / pear
f gun / pow / der
g un / a / void / a / ble
h co / in / ci / dence
i in / sen / si / tive
2 **a** def / in / ite (3)
b prac / tise (2)
c cap / size (2)
d en / ter / prise (3)
e op / po / site (3)
f ex / er / cise (3)
3 **1** prune **2** apple **3** banana **4** miscalculate **5** electricity

(35) Prefixes 3 p46
1 **a** antidote **b** exchange **c** coincidence **d** anticlockwise
e antibiotic **f** export **g** antisocial **h** exit
2 **a** misbehave **b** non-fiction **c** miscalculate **d** misread
e non-stick **f** non-starter **g** miscount **h** misfortune
3 **a** exhale **b** antiseptic **c** explain **d** misheard
e co-starring **f** mistake

(36) Homonyms p47
1 Homonyms: **a** watch **c** club **d** form **f** block
Not homonyms: **b** knee **e** door **g** girl **h** hat
2 jam: a sticky spread made from fruit / blocking a road with traffic
leaves: to go away / they grow on a tree
train: a series of railway carriages / to get ready for a race
3 **a** fly / fly **b** table / table **c** bark / bark
4 **a** row / row **b** read / read **c** sow / sow **d** wound / wound

(37) Synonyms p48
1 **a** asked / enquired / queried **b** wondered / supposed / guessed
c cried / wailed / howled **d** laughed / giggled / smirked
2 Possible answers include:
a screamed / screeched / squealed
b remarked / stated / mentioned **c** stammered / mumbled / murmured
3 Possible answers include: shouted / yelled / whispered / snarled / whimpered

(38) Using a dictionary p49
1 **a** 2nd **b** 4th **c** 3rd **d** 2nd **e** 4th
2 Friday / Monday / Saturday / Sunday / Tuesday / Wednesday
3 **a** gable / gentle / gnome / gobble / gulp
b obstinate / olive / opposite / otter / oval
c sack / scarf / should / snowflake / submerge

(39) Personal pronouns p50
1 **a** she / it **b** they / They **c** We **d** I / her / we
2 he: Henry / John / Matthew
she: Amelia / Carrie / Penny
we: Dad and I / Rick and I / Una and I
they: Tom and Joe / Grandma and Granddad / Helen and Zoe
3 **a** He / them / they **b** We / it **c** He / her / it
d It

(40) Possessive pronouns p51
1 **a** his **b** ours / yours **c** Their / hers **d** Our / theirs
2 **a** his **b** her **c** mine **d** my **e** ours
3 **a** you / yours **b** my / yours **c** me / mine **d** their / Ours

(41) Conjunctions p52
1 **a** so **b** since **c** until **d** while
2 **a** after **b** as **c** or **d** when
3 Answers will vary.

(42) 1st, 2nd and 3rd person 2 p53
1 Walk out of the front door and down the garden path. Go through the gate and turn left onto Maple Avenue. At the end of the road turn left and walk past the Post Office on your left and the bank on your right. Cross the road at the crossing outside the newsagents and then walk almost to the end of the road. The school is on the right. Walk through the gates and round the back of the school to the playground.
2 Answers will vary.

(43) Signalling time p54
1 **a** 2, 1, 3 **b** 2, 1, 3
2 Firstly, write your address in the top right hand corner.
Secondly, put the name and address of the person to whom you are writing on the left hand side.
After the addresses, write, 'Dear Sir or Madam'.
Once you have done this, you can write the text of your letter.
Before you put your name, write 'Yours faithfully' underneath the last paragraph.
Lastly, sign your name.

(44) Contractions 2 p55
1 **a** Who's **b** There's **c** What's / haven't
d That's **e** weren't
2 **a** salt and vinegar **b** shall not **c** mix and match
d tell them **e** madam **f** fish and chips

3

	Full	Contracted	Full	Contracted
	could not	couldn't	What will	What'll
	It is	It's	Who would have	Who would've / Who'd have
	should have	should've	would not	wouldn't
	will not	won't	is not	isn't

(45) Punctuating speech p56
1 **a** "How late are you going to be?" Jody asked.
b "What do you want for your tea tonight?" Mum enquired.
c "Becky, where are you?" called Toby.
d "Did you hear that?" asked Jonny.
2 **a** "Help!" cried the little boy.
b "That is amazing!" replied Abdul.
c "I am going to the library and will meet my brother there."
d "We are going to get a cat from the rescue centre because we want a pet."
3 **a** Fawzia turned round and shouted, "I will see you later."
b "Do you have to go already?" asked Ben.
c "Look out!" shrieked Debbie. "That bucket nearly fell on you!"

(46) Commas 2 p57
1 **a** While I was eating, the dog played in the garden.
b When the rain stops, we'll go shopping.
c As he took a long time to get ready, he was late for school.
d If you are ill, you really should go to the doctor.
2 **a** "James, I told you to come straight home after school!"
b No comma
c No comma
d "Marcus, please don't do that!"
3 **a** Yes, the train will arrive on time.
b If you don't eat your dinner, you can't have pudding.
c Having finally finished the exam, he was allowed to leave the room.
d Phillip, what is behind the door?

(47) Understanding a story p58
1 In Japanese woodland
2 2
3 He got caught in a noose
4 A passing traveller
5 He turned into a tea-kettle
6 He was jumping about wildly.
7 Because he'd been skipping in and out of the gorse bushes.
8 **a** The badger rolled over and over down the hill.
b The badger got caught in a noose.
c The badger transformed himself into a tea-kettle.
9 Possible answers inlcude:
So that the traveller could make himself a cup of tea.

(48) Formal letters p60
1 a solicitor
2 someone who has employed you to do a job
3 company
4 bothering someone
5 To sue for damages.
6 Possible answers include:
on behalf of our client, does not cease, we must inform you, Yours sincerely
7 Paragraphs in a word-processed letter are not indented. When a letter is hand-written, the first line of each new paragraph is indented.
8 Paragraph 1 explains why Harold Meeny is writing the letter.
Paragraph 2 explains what happens.
Paragraph 3 introduces a separate subject.
9 Yes. The letterhead shows the company name is, Meeny Miny Mo & Co., so Harold Meeny must be a partner or director in the company.
10 The letter does not say. Harold Meeny has written a formal letter on behalf of his clients, so his own opinions are not expressed.

How am I doing? p62
1 **a** critic / it / tic **b** art / if **c** object **d** miser / is / era / able
2 **a** con / junc / tions **b** syl / la / bles **c** ex / er / cise **d** def / i / ni / tions
3 **a** misbehave **b** non-stop **c** miscalculate **d** misfire
e nonsense **f** non-smoker **g** non-drip **h** misfortune
4 Homonyms: star book hard watch play
Not homonyms: stairs photo birthday boy maths
5 asked / enquired whispered / murmured cried / wailed
laughed / giggled shouted / yelled
6 Friday / Monday / Saturday / Sunday / Thursday / Tuesday / Wednesday
7 **a** He went to town. **b** They went to Kent.
8 Possible answers include: **a** my / my **b** your **c** theirs
9 **a** so **b** but **c** before
10 **a** third peson **b** first person
11 2, 1, 3
12 **a** wouldn't **b** that's **c** he's
d mustn't **e** they've **f** I'll
13 **a** While I was eating, the cat chased a mouse.
b OK, if you think that's a good idea.
14 **a** "Not now!" Mum said crossly. "Wait until I've finished dinner."
b "I'm bored!" moaned Shelly. "What can we do now?"

Essential words

> Some words in sentences are **essential**. If you took them out either the sentence **wouldn't make any sense** or it could **change the meaning** of the sentence.
> - I ____ football.   Without the **verb**, a sentence does not make sense.
> - I play _____.   Without the **noun**, the sentence still makes sense but you don't know what game is being played.
>
> Removing **adjectives** from sentences is less likely to alter the meaning than if you missed out a verb.

1. **Underline the verbs and cross out the adjectives.**   *(13 marks)*

   When I go to school in the early morning I have to remember to take my

   lunchbox and blue flask with me. On Tuesday, Mum reminds me to take my PE

   kit, but I only need my football boots on Wednesday. It is my favourite sport

   in the whole world.

2. **Read the paragraph again leaving out all the adjectives. Which adjective has to stay in so that the sentence keeps its sense?**

   _____

3. **Underline the five main pieces of information in this passage. Cross out the words you do not need but keep the meaning of the sentences.**   *(5 marks)*

   Last summer I went to Spain with my Mum and Uncle Henry, my brother

   Simon and sister Benita. My whole family went! It was so hot, I was boiling

   and the sun shone every day. It was great to go swimming in the cool, blue

   sea but Benita just preferred to sunbathe on the beach.

0	Tough	OK	Got it!	19

Total
/19

More practice? Go to www

1st, 2nd and 3rd person 1

When you write from **your own point of view** it is called writing in the **first person**.

   I went to the shops.   **We** went to the shops.

When you talk **directly to someone** it is called the **second person**.

   You can't park there.

When you write about **what someone else is doing** it is called writing in the **third person**.

   Sam went to the shops.   **They** went to the shops.

1. **Write whether these sentences are written in the first, second or third person.**

   a They cheered very loudly. _third person_____

   b Would you like an ice cream? _____

   c We played hockey in our PE lesson today. _____

   d I can't decide what to wear! _____

   e You must hand in your homework tomorrow. _____

   f David invited John to his party. _____

2. **Change these sentences from the third person to the first person.**

   a Ashen and Ben took the dog for a walk.

   _____

   b Isabel got dressed for school very quickly.

   _____

   c Oliver fed the ducks in the park.

   _____

   d Bethan and Lauren took turns to use the computer.

   _____

0			q
Tough	OK	Got it!	

Total

/q

More practice? Go to www

> **Commas** are used to separate a list of items when they are written in a sentence. The word **and** or **or** is written before the last item instead of a comma.
>
> His Mum packed him a shirt, a pair of trousers, some socks **and** a toothbrush.

1. **Put commas into these sentences.**

  a It was a tall dark and gloomy house.

  b Mark crunched his way across the cold frosty and sparkling field.

  c Zoe had a furry cuddly bear for her birthday.

2. **This time put in the word 'and' as well as the commas.**

  a The train called at Sunbury Hampton Fulwell.

  b The leaves in autumn are red yellow gold brown.

  c Butter flour sugar a pinch of salt were the recipe's ingredients.

3. **Write the passage out underneath, putting in commas and the words 'and' or 'or' where they are needed.** *(6 marks)*

Lucas had lost Oscar. "Is he at the Town Hall the station the shops?" wondered Lucas. He tried the Town Hall the bus terminus last of all the market to find him. He found him sitting quietly by the fish stall. Oscar was eating a chunk of cod a piece of haddock some salmon!

_____

_____

_____

_____

_____

			Total
0 Tough	OK	Got it! 12	/12

Capital letters

Capital letters have several jobs. We have already seen that they are used at the **start of sentences**, for the first word of **direct speech** and for **proper nouns**.

They are also used:

- to begin the **most important** words in **headings**.
  Chapter **O**ne: **T**he **B**eginning of **L**ife
- for **adjectives** formed from proper nouns. **G**eorgian
- at the start of each **new line in a poem**. **H**ere I am,
  Here I be.
  I can see you
  But you can't see me!

1. **Underline the letters in these headings which should have capital letters.**

   a section 3: the history of the human race.

   b table of contents.

   c act 1 scene 1: pandora's house.

2. **Circle the letters which should be capitals.**

   a "I would not have liked living in elizabethan times," commented Jackie.

   b "What accent is that? Oh, of course, it is a liverpudlian accent."

   c The school established an exchange programme with an african school.

   d Ruth and Gareth went out to a japanese restaurant for dinner.

   e Roast beef and all the trimmings is Amanda's favourite british meal.

3. **Write this four-line poem correctly, putting in all the capital letters.** (4 marks)

   charlie junior, a small baboon, went outside in the great monsoon. when he got home he started to sneeze and the shivers and shakes went down to his knees.

   _____

   _____

   _____

   _____

0			12
Tough	OK	Got it!	

Total

12

More practice? Go to www

Contractions 1

A **contraction** is where two words have been **joined** together and some of the letters have been **left out**. An **apostrophe** is used to show this.

I **ha**d = I'd   he **is** = he's   they **are** = they're   it **is** or it **was** = it's

There are some irregular contractions and these must be learnt.

I will not = **I won't**   you shall not = you **shan't**
they would = **they'd**   who would have = **who'd have** or **who would've**

1. **Write the contractions for these words.**

   a you had _____   **b** she had _____   **c** they had _____

   d I have _____   **e** you have _____   **f** she has _____

   g I will _____   **h** they will _____   **i** you will _____

2. **Join each phrase with its contraction.**

   they'll   it does not   we are   I had not   I am   they shouldn't

   we're   I'm   it doesn't   they should not   they will   I hadn't

3. **Complete these sentences with the contractions of the words in brackets.**

   a "You ___needn't___ worry, _____ be there on time." (need not / she will)

   b "_____ the shop. The directions _____ easy to follow." (Here is / were not)

   c I _____ invited to the party, so I _____ go. (was not / can not)

   d "You _____ done that! _____ wrong!" (should not have / It is)

   e I wanted to know _____ been in the car in front of me. (who had)

   f "_____ you going to invite me in now _____ here?" (are not / I am)

   g It says _____ dangerous, so we _____ go in the water. (it is / must not)

			Total
0 Tough	OK	Got it! 17	/17

More practice? Go to www

37

Adventure stories

> All good stories have a clear pattern. They have:
> * an **opening** that introduces the people, place and time
> * a **problem** in the middle
> * a **solution** at the end.

The Wrong Path

It was sunny when Harry the dog decided to go for a walk. "I know I'm not supposed to go by myself, but it'll only be for a few minutes," he said.

Harry trotted through the wood, his four paws carrying him swiftly along the leaf-strewn path. Soon the path became narrower and the trees seemed to lean in towards him. "I think I'll go home now," whispered Harry to himself. But it was so dark he couldn't see the path anymore. Then a large, heavy drop of rain dripped onto Harry's nose. Soon the rain was pouring down. Harry was cold and scared. He lifted up his little furry head and howled.

"Good gracious!" said a voice. "Is that little Harry?" It was Dr Gordon carrying a large umbrella. "I think I'd better take you home," said Dr Gordon.

Carefully, he tucked Harry under his arm. Soon they were safely home in Harry's garden. "Now don't go running off again!" said Dr Gordon.

Harry wagged his tail. He didn't want to run away ever again!

1. Circle the correct answers to these questions.

a Where does the story take place?

In a garden   In a wood   In a town

b How many characters are there in the story?

two   one   four   three   five

c What is Harry's main problem?

He doesn't know the way home   He has taken the wrong path

He can't see the path

d Who helps him?

A stranger   His owner   A doctor

e What does Harry do when he gets home?

He says thank you   He wags his tail   He runs away again

2. Do you think Dr Gordon had met Harry before. Why?

_____

3. Write down three things the story tells us about the wood. *(3 marks)*

   a _____

   b _____

   c _____

4. Summarise the main points of the story in sequence from each paragraph.

(3 marks)

   a Harry went for a walk. _____

   b _____

   c _____

   d _____

5. Do you think Harry was brave or foolish to go for a walk? Why?

_____

6. How do you think he felt when he couldn't see the path home? Why?

_____

7. What lesson do you think Harry has learnt by the end of the story?

_____

			Total
0 Tough	OK	Got it! 15	15

More practice? Go to www

Instructions

Read these instructions for making a kaleidoscope. Then answer the questions.

1 You will need a cylinder of cardboard. You can make one or use a ready-made box or tube.

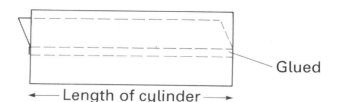

Glued

←— Length of cylinder —→

2 Card to fit into cylinder. Use shiny or reflective card for best results.

3 Fold to make a Y-shaped profile and insert into cylinder.

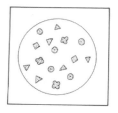 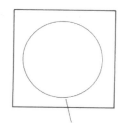

Draw circles the same size as cylinder onto two pieces of grease-proof paper.

4 You need coloured shapes such as sequins. Glue carefully round the edges of the circles and place together trapping the sequins between the circles in a 'sandwich'.

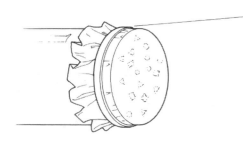

5 Use an elastic band to fasten the double layer of grease-proof paper to the tube.

6 Hold to light and look down the tube to see the colours. Rotate the tube.

1. How many steps are there in making a kaleidoscope?_____

2. List the things you need to make a kaleidoscope.

    _____

    _____

3. Into what shape do you need to fold the card inside the tube?

    _____

4. What is the best card to use inside the tube?

    _____

5. How do you fix the grease-proof paper to the tube?

    _____

6. What do you think creates the coloured patterns in the kaleidoscope?

    _____

7. How do you operate the kaleidoscope?

    _____

8. Would it be easy or hard to make the kaleidoscope from these instructions?
    Can you explain why?

    _____

    _____

Tough	OK	Got it!	

0   8

Total
8

More practice? Go to www

How am I doing?

1. Add the endings er and est to these words.   *(3 marks, $^1/_2$ mark for each)*

	er	est
a fresh		
b ripe		
c friendly		

2. Add the suffix y to these words.

a smoke _____   **b** crisp _____   **c** full _____

d stone _____   **e** water _____   **f** bone _____

3. Write the plural of these words.

a dish _____   **b** mouse _____   **c** foot _____

d penny _____   **e** halo _____   **f** taxi _____

4. Underline the silent letters in these words.

a wren   **b** plumber   **c** sword   **d** gnat   **e** knife

f calm   **g** would   **h** rhythm   **i** hedge   **j** knuckle

5. Write two compound words that start with each of the words below.   *(4 marks)*

a sand   _____   _____

b bed   _____   _____

c book   _____   _____

d side   _____   _____

6. Add the suffix ly, ful or less to these words to complete the sentences.

beauty   power   coward

a She looked _____ in her new dress.

b Sir John was a _____ knight who didn't like battles.

c I am _____ to do anything.

7. Choose interesting adjectives to complete these sentences.

a The _____, _____ lady wore a _____, _____ dress.

b It was a _____, _____ day.

8. **Change these sentences from singular to plural.**

   a The man enjoys watching comedy films.

   _____

   b Justin thinks skateboarding is fun but he prefers watching it on TV.

   _____

9. **Circle the collective nouns in these sentences.**

   a The light shower of rain didn't stop the team playing well. The crowd roared their approval and the best player was given a bouquet of flowers at the end.

   b There was a long queue in the bakery because a new batch of bread had been prepared.

   c Jon wanted to show Mark his collection of stamps but Mark preferred to watch the programme on the African tribes.

10. **Write whether these sentences are written in the first, second or third person.**

   a Matthew really enjoyed reading that book. _____

   b Stop doing that – both of you! _____

   c After school, they walked home carrying their books. _____

   d We are going on holiday to Spain next week. _____

11. **Write in the word 'and' and any commas where they are missing.**

   a Today   has   been   wet   miserable   horrible.

   b Jack's   puppy   was   cute   friendly   .funny.

12. **Write the contractions for these words.**

   a need not _____   **b** will not _____   **c** there is _____

   d you will _____   **e** who had _____   **f** I would _____

Total

51

More practice? Go to www

Words inside words

Seeing **words inside bigger words** helps you to spell them. When you look at a new word ask yourself, "Which bit do I already know? Is there another word hiding inside it?"

scowl = sc-**owl**   season = **sea-son**

1. **Choose one of these two-letter words to complete the words below:**

   on   **an**   **in**

   a m __ __ ey   **b** d __ __ key   **c** f __ __ cy   **d** husb __ __ d

   e s __ __ d   **f** s __ __ gle   **g** m __ __ imal   **h** s __ __ ger

2. **Underline any two or three-letter words you find inside the words below.**

   Many words have smaller words hidden inside them. Finding them helps you with your spelling, especially if they are long or difficult.

   a How many two-letter words did you find? _____

   b How many three-letter words did you find? _____

3. **Without rearranging the letters, find as many words inside words as you can.**

   a falling _____   **b** splendid _____

   c finale _____   **d** hindrance _____

   e abundance _____   **f** admittance _____

   g supplement _____   **h** fantastic _____

   i obsession _____   **j** centimetre _____

   k potatoes _____   **l** another _____

0			22
Tough	OK	Got it!	

Total

22

More practice? Go to www